Jesus Loves Everybody:
Especially Me

⯈

Coloring Book

By Nicole Benoit-Roy
Illustrated by Joshua Allen

authorHOUSE®

AuthorHouse™
1663 Liberty Drive
Bloomington, IN 47403
www.authorhouse.com
Phone: 1-800-839-8640

First published by AuthorHouse   11/21/2011

ISBN: 978-1-4685-0123-0 (sc)
ISBN: 978-1-4685-0122-3 (ebk)

Library of Congress Control Number: 2011961381

Printed in the United States of America

Any people depicted in stock imagery provided by Thinkstock are models, and such images are being used for illustrative purposes only.
Certain stock imagery © Thinkstock.

This book is printed on acid-free paper.

Because of the dynamic nature of the Internet, any web addresses or links contained in this book may have changed since publication and may no longer be valid. The views expressed in this work are solely those of the author and do not necessarily reflect the views of the publisher, and the publisher hereby disclaims any responsibility for them.

Contents

Jesus Loves Me

All About My Needs

&

"And my God will meet all your needs according to his glorious riches in Christ Jesus." Philippians 4:19, LASB

Jesus loves me

when I am hungry.

Jesus loves me

enough to give me food.

Jesus loves me

when I am sick.

Jesus loves me

enough to heal me.

Jesus loves me

when I am upset.

Jesus loves me

enough to comfort me.

Jesus' love makes me glad,

and I know it.

Jesus Loves You
All About Meal Time

&

"Give us today our daily bread."
Matthew 6:11, LASB

Jesus loves you

while you're eating breakfast.

Jesus loves you

while you're eating brunch.

Jesus loves you

while you're eating lunch.

Jesus loves you

while you're eating dinner.

Jesus loves you,

even while you're eating a snack.

Jesus Loves My Mommy

All About Location

ॐ

"Make level paths for your feet and take only ways that are firm."

Proverbs 4:26, LASB

Jesus loves my mommy

when she is at home.

Jesus loves my mommy

when she is at work.

Jesus loves my mommy

when she is at church.

Jesus loves my mommy

when she is at the supermarket.

Jesus loves my mommy

when she is at the mall.

I love my mommy,

because Jesus loves her first.

Jesus Loves My Daddy
All About Responsibility

"Fathers, do not exasperate your children; instead, bring them up in the training and instruction of the Lord."

Ephesians 6:4, LASB

Jesus loves my daddy

when he reads to me.

Jesus loves my daddy

when he swims with me.

Jesus loves my daddy

when he takes me to church.

Jesus loves my daddy

when he prays with me.

Jesus loves my daddy

when he loves mommy.

Jesus loves my daddy all the time,

and he knows it.